America at WAR

World WAR II

TEN GREATEST BATTLES

John Perritano

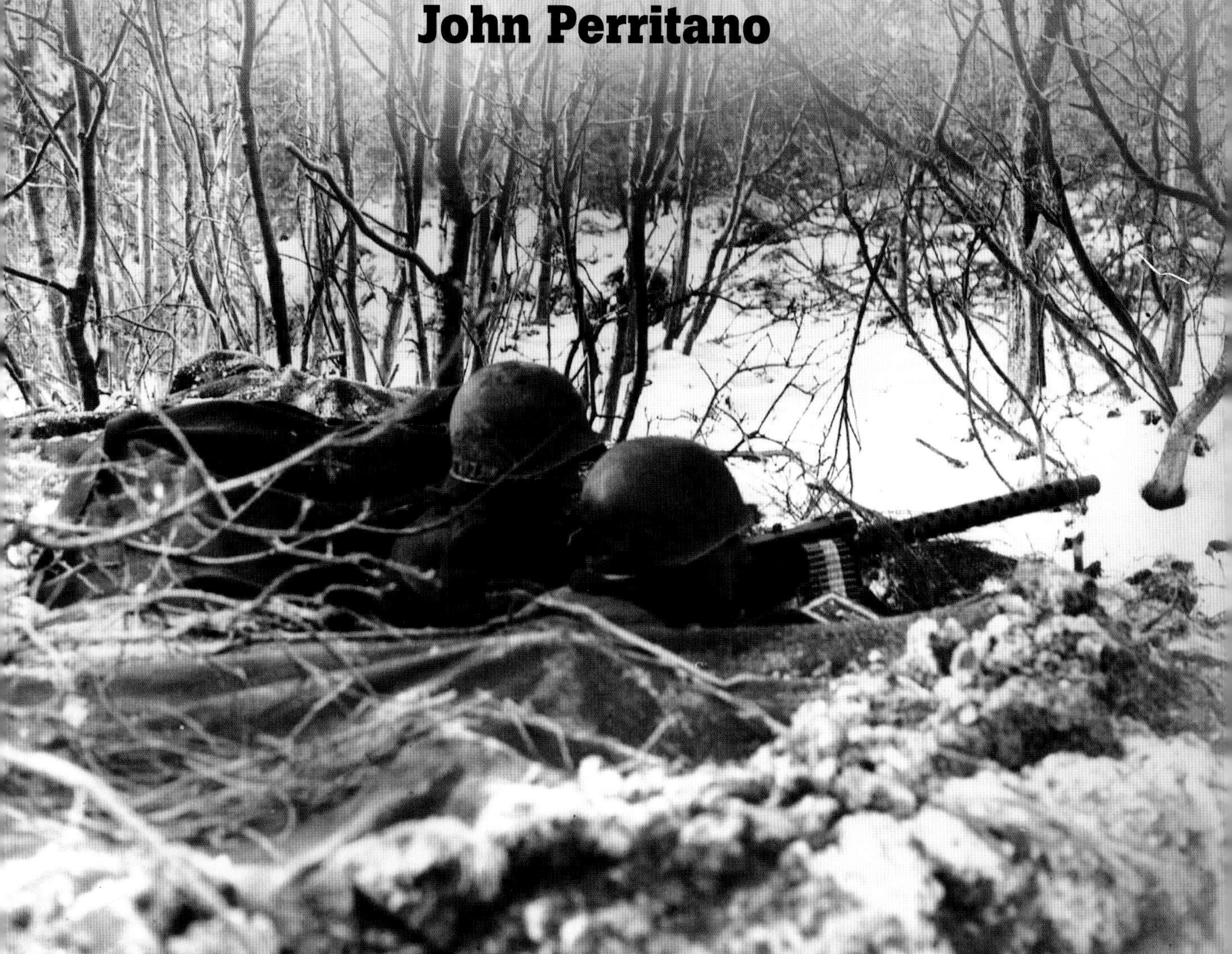

Created by Q2AMedia
www.q2amedia.com

Editor Jessica Cohn
Publishing Director Chester Fisher
Client Service Manager Sujatha Menon
Project Manager Kumar Kunal
Art Director Joita Das
Designer Parul Gambhir
Picture Researchers Debarata Sen and Anju Pathak

10 9 8 7 6 5 4 3 2 1

ISBN10: 81-907857-5-3
ISBN13: 978-81-907857-5-4

Printed in China

Picture Credits
t= top, b= bottom, c= centre, r= right, l= left

Cover Page: US-Army history images
Back Cover: Hendrickson (Army)
Title Page: U.S. Army Center of Military History
Imprint Page: AP Photo
Half Title: Associated Press.

4-5 AFP. 4t Library of Congress Prints and Photographs Division Washington, D.C. 20540 USA. 4b Topical Press Agency: Getty Images. 6-7 Hulton Archive: Getty Images. 6 Lapi: Roger Viollet: Getty Images. 7 AP Photo. 8 AP Photo. 9t Library of Congress Prints and Photographs Division Washington, D.C. 20540 USA. 9b New Times Paris Bureau Collection.(USIA). 10-11 Bettmann: Corbis. 10 Keystone: Getty Images. 12-13 Central Press: Hulton Archive: Getty Images. 12 U.S. Navy Photo. 13 AP Photo. 14 Roger Viollet: Getty Images. 15t Keystone: Getty Images. 15b Library of Congress Prints and Photographs Division Washington, D.C. 20540 USA. 16-17 Hulton Archive: Getty Images. 18 National Archives and Records Administration. 19t National Archives and Records Administration. 19b Hulton Archive: Getty Images. 20-21 U.S. Army Center Of Military History. 21 T4C Messerlin. 22-23 Cphom Robert F. Sargent. 23 AP Photo. 24 U.S. Army Center of Military History. 25t U.S. Army Center of Military History. 25b AP Photo. 26 U.S. Army Center of Military History. 27t U.S. Army Center of Military History. 27b Library of Congress. 28 Ivan Shagin: Getty Images 29 Superstock Inc: Photolibrary. 30 Photo Courtesy of U.S. Army. 31 National Archives and Records Administration.

Q2AMedia Art Bank: 5, 11, 17, 21

Contents

Battle of France

Germany's surprise invasion of Poland on September 1, 1939, marked the beginning of World War II. Poland had a half million soldiers ready to fight—and even more in the reserves. Yet, they were no match for the powerful German army.

Adolf Hitler, chancellor of Germany

Poland surrendered on September 28, allowing Germany's dictator, Adolf Hitler, to turn his attention toward Western Europe. Britain and France had declared war on Germany just two days after the Nazis marched into Poland. However, neither **Allied** country was prepared to stop Germany.

After conquering Poland, Hitler claimed that he wanted peace with other nations. But Hitler was lying. He was stalling for time to get his forces rested for his next target, France.

Parisians follow the news of the German advance.

Plan of Attack

Commander:	Generalfeldmarschall Erich von Manstein (Germany)
Tactics:	Conquer France and advance to the English Channel
Where:	Western Europe
When:	May–June 1940

Nazis Advance

Great Britain sent a small army across the English Channel to try to slow the German march across Western Europe. But the Nazis were too well prepared and powerful to be stopped. By June of 1940, Germany had conquered Denmark, Norway, Belgium, the Netherlands, and Luxembourg. France was next.

Line of Defense

The French were feeling a false sense of security. They had built a "chain" of concrete, steel, and other fortifications, known as the Maginot Line, after World War I (1914–1918). The Maginot Line was an obstacle for the Germans. The fortifications stretched across France's border with Germany. But German General Erich von Manstein had a clever plan. Instead of assaulting the Maginot Line directly, as the French expected, the Germans would go *around* it.

More than a million German soldiers pour into Poland.

Battle of France

North and South

The Germans divided their forces. A small army marched through northern Belgium, which served as a distraction. A much larger force plowed through the Ardennes Forest in southern Belgium.

The two-fisted attack took Britain and France by surprise. Most of the Allied troops were in northern Belgium, where they believed the fighting would take place. Nazi tanks and planes cut through the middle of the Allied armies, steamrolling into France.

The German air force, the Luftwaffe, bombed roads and bridges as Nazi troops advanced. German **paratroopers** dropped from airplanes behind enemy lines. The Allies were forced to retreat to the English Channel.

In July 1940, the Germans sweep into Paris.

German soldiers advance in Panzers.

Weapons of War: Panzer

The Nazis developed a tank called a Panzer. Its name came from the German word for "armor" or "turtle shell." Panzers were armed with cannons and machine guns. These German weapons were used to great advantage during the Battle of France.

Trapped at Dunkirk

By late May 1940, German forces had trapped thousands of British and French soldiers near Dunkirk, a seaport in northern France. The Allies had their backs to the sea. The Germans were ready for the kill. Then Hitler made a major mistake. He ordered his Panzers to stop advancing. Instead, he directed the Luftwaffe to finish off the Allies. But the German air force could not do the job.

By the time the German tanks started to roll again, heavy rain made their attack more difficult. This gave the Allies in England the chance they needed to rescue their troops at Dunkirk by sea. Thousands of Allied soldiers escaped aboard hundreds of ships.

The good news for the Allies did not last long, however. Determined Nazi forces continued to move toward Paris. On June 14, German troopers marched into the city. The French government surrendered on June 22. In defeating France, Germany had swept away the Allied resistance in mainland Western Europe.

At Dunkirk, Allied soldiers are saved by ships.

Battle of Britain

With France and most of Europe now under Nazi *occupation*, Germany planned to cross the English Channel and invade Great Britain. The Nazi code name for the invasion was "Operation Sea Lion."

German dive bombers take to the skies in August 1940.

Plan of Attack

Commander:	Reichsmarschall Hermann Goering (Germany)
Tactics:	Win control of English airspace
Where:	Skies over Great Britain
When:	July–September 1940

Before Operation Sea Lion could begin, Hitler ordered the Luftwaffe to gain control of the air over Great Britain. "The English Air Force must be so reduced . . . that it is unable to deliver any significant attack against the German crossing," Hitler ordered.

The job of destroying the Royal Air Force (RAF) fell to Hermann Goering, head of the Luftwaffe. On July 10, 1940, the Luftwaffe attacked several British targets, including ships in the English Channel. The Battle of Britain had begun.

The Upper Hand

Every day, German planes targeted British airfields and other military bases. Although outnumbered by the enemy, British pilots earned the upper hand. They won many **dogfights**.

The RAF commander was Air Chief Marshal Sir Hugh Dowding. He ordered attacks on German planes before they could do much damage. The British used a new invention called **radar**. This technology allowed the RAF to track German planes in the sky. The tactic worked. By the middle of September, the Luftwaffe had lost thousands of planes and crew members. British planes then **counterattacked**, bombing German cities, including the capital, Berlin.

With the battle slipping from his fingers, Goering ordered mass bombings of London and other British cities. But by October the German air attacks had diminished. The Battle of Britain was over. The Germans put a halt to their plans for invasion.

Hermann Goering, leader of the Luftwaffe

In Command: Hermann Goering

Although Hermann Goering had been a World War I flying ace, he did not have any experience commanding aircraft in war.

British firefighters attempt to keep the damage under control.

Pearl Harbor

December 7, 1941, seemed like just another Sunday morning at the U.S. Naval Base at Pearl Harbor, on the island of Oahu, Hawaii. Sailors and soldiers sat down to breakfast or dressed for worship services.

At around 7:55 A.M., Japanese warplanes attacked the American fleet by surprise. The Japanese had sent six aircraft carriers with more than 420 planes to destroy the U.S. forces. The carriers were accompanied by a large number of battleships, cruisers, and destroyers. It was one of the largest carrier **task forces** ever assembled.

The planes flew in from the south. U.S. sailors thought the incoming planes were American until they saw the red circles on the wings. The red "meatball," as U.S. troops called it, was the symbol of the "rising sun" of the Empire of Japan.

Japan's sunrise assault came in two waves. There were 183 aircraft in the first wave, including torpedo bombers, dive bombers, and fighter planes.

Japanese torpedo planes, like this one, are sent on the surprise attack.

Plan of Attack

Commander: Admiral Isoroku Yamamoto (Japan)

Tactics: Destroy the U.S. Pacific Fleet

Where: Pearl Harbor, Hawaii

Date: December 7, 1941

Second Wave

The second wave shot up U.S. airfields on Oahu before reaching the American fleet at anchor. Explosion after explosion ripped through the ships. Torpedoes and bombs sank the battleship *West Virginia*.

Torpedoes blasted holes in the battleship *Oklahoma*, trapping hundreds of people below decks. The ship capsized within minutes, killing 429. When the battleship *Arizona* blew up, it took 1,177 sailors and Marines to watery graves.

When the attack was over at 9:55 A.M., more than 2,400 people had died. The U.S. Pacific Fleet had been heavily damaged. A day later, the United States declared war on Japan.

The *U.S.S. California* comes under attack.

In Command: Admiral Isoroku Yamamoto

In 1941, Japan expanded its empire in Southeast Asia. In response, the U.S. cut off oil supplies to Japan. That led Admiral Isoroku Yamamoto to devise a secret plan to attack Pearl Harbor and destroy the American fleet.

This map shows where the ships of the U.S. Pacific Fleet were anchored on December 7, 1941.

Battle of the Atlantic

The Battle of the Atlantic began on September 3, 1939, and ran throughout the war. In this battle on the seas, Britain fought for its very survival.

The Germans used submarines, known as U-boats, to prevent ships from carrying food, troops, tanks, and other supplies to the British Isles. The battle began when the first U-boat sank the first British ship. The passenger liner *Athenia* was steaming for Canada with more than 1,100 passengers, including 311 Americans. A German sub fired a torpedo at the ship, killing 112 people. Although heavily damaged, *Athenia* remained afloat, and the survivors were rescued. But the German navy stalked British shipping from that day forward.

The Germans used U-boats, underwater explosives, airplanes, and warships to sink millions of tons of shipping during the last half of 1940. At the height of its naval power, Germany had 200 U-boats prowling the Atlantic.

Balloons float over British ships, protecting them from enemy aircraft.

A U.S. crew tows a captured German U-boat in 1944.

Plan of Attack

Commander:	Admiral Karl Dönitz (Germany)
Tactics:	Stop supplies from reaching Great Britain
Where:	Atlantic Ocean
Date:	1939–1945

U-boat crew members line up for roll call.

Gaining Control

The British had some success sinking Nazi warships, such as the mighty *Bismarck* battleship. But the U-boats were more difficult to destroy. The subs traveled together in **wolfpacks**. Groups of submarines surfaced and attacked at the same time.

The Allies regained control of the waters by sending warships along with their merchant vessels. When U-boats attacked, airplanes from the warships went into action, forcing the subs deep below the sea. New anti-submarine weapons destroyed many U-boats as well. According to some sources, the Allies were able to sink at least 45 German subs in 1945.

German Admiral Karl Dönitz called off the battle on May 23, 1943. The threat of isolated U-boat attacks continued until the end of the war, however.

Weapons of War: The *Bismarck*

The Nazi battleship *Bismarck*, named after former German Chancellor Otto von Bismarck, was the pride of the German navy. The 41,673-ton battleship seemed indestructible. The *Bismarck* was able to destroy the British battle cruiser *Hood* in the Battle of Denmark Strait on May 24, 1941. But as the German ship was heading back to occupied France for repairs, the British sank it. The *Bismarck* went down on May 27, killing most of the crew.

Stalingrad

On June 22, 1941, some 3 million German troops, armed with tanks, *artillery*, and aircraft, launched a surprise attack on the Soviet Union.

The Germans struck with lightning speed. They captured hundreds of thousands of unprepared Soviet troops. Hitler believed his army would destroy the Soviets in short order. But the Germans soon faced freezing winter weather. They had to battle huge snowdrifts and icy conditions.

Members of Germany's Sixth Army move in on the city of Stalingrad.

Plan of Attack

Commander: Generalfeldmarschall Friedrich Paulus (Germany)
Tactics: Capture Stalingrad
Where: Stalingrad, Soviet Union
Date: July 1942–February 1943

In spring 1942, German troops pressed toward Stalingrad, a strategic Soviet city on the Volga River. Stalingrad, named for Soviet leader Josef Stalin, was an important industrial city and the gateway to the oil-rich Caucasus region. Hitler needed the oil to fuel the Nazi war machine. Leading the German campaign was General Friedrich Paulus, who pushed toward the city in June and July.

Fatal Mistake

Paulus might have taken the city. However, Hitler ordered his commander to send one part of the army south to the Caucasus. He ordered the other part north to Stalingrad. By splitting the army, the Germans lost their chance.

On August 23, 1942, the tip of the German army reached the Volga River north of Stalingrad. Other units moved to places just outside the city. German planes, artillery, and tanks reduced much of the city to rubble.

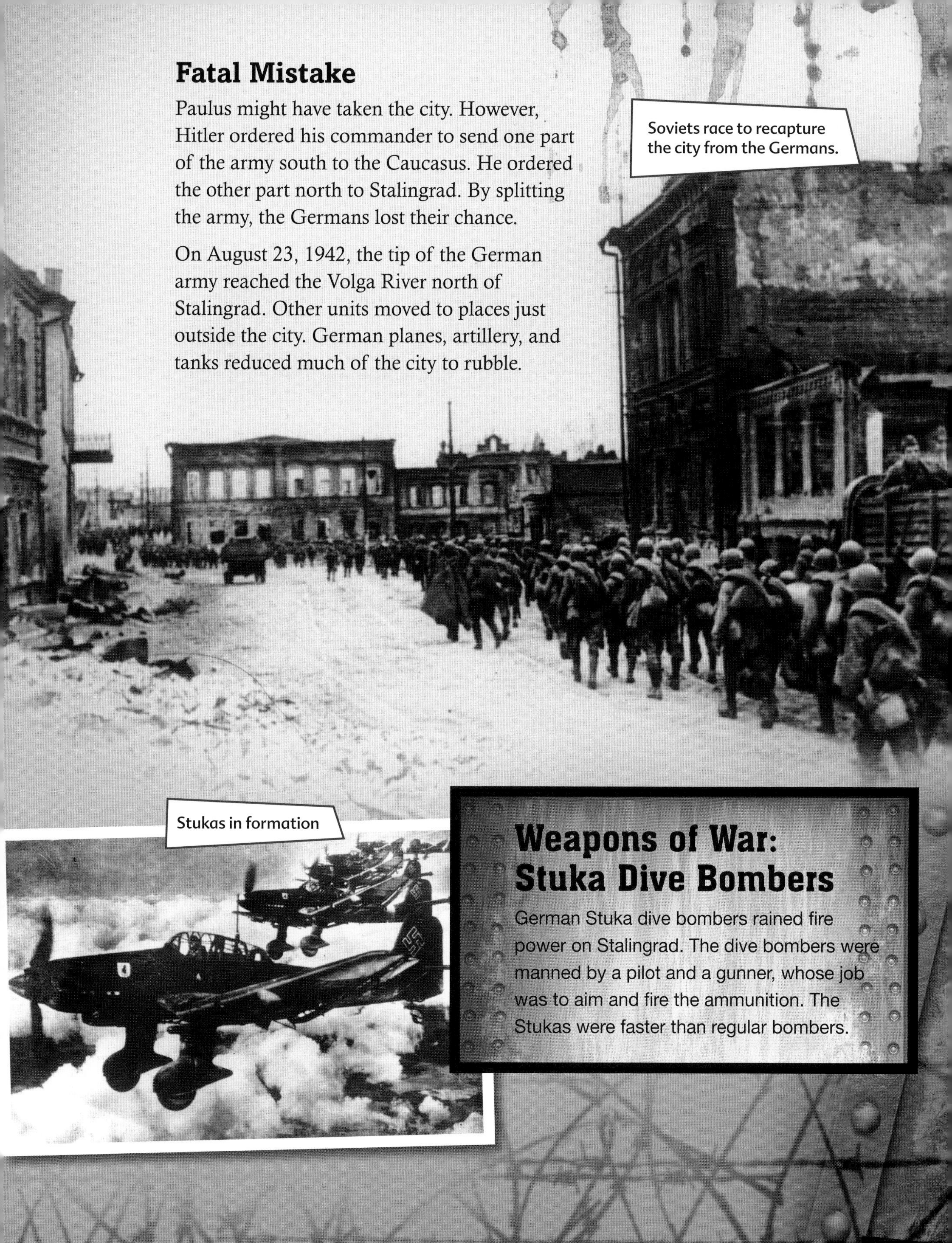

Soviets race to recapture the city from the Germans.

Stukas in formation

Weapons of War: Stuka Dive Bombers

German Stuka dive bombers rained fire power on Stalingrad. The dive bombers were manned by a pilot and a gunner, whose job was to aim and fire the ammunition. The Stukas were faster than regular bombers.

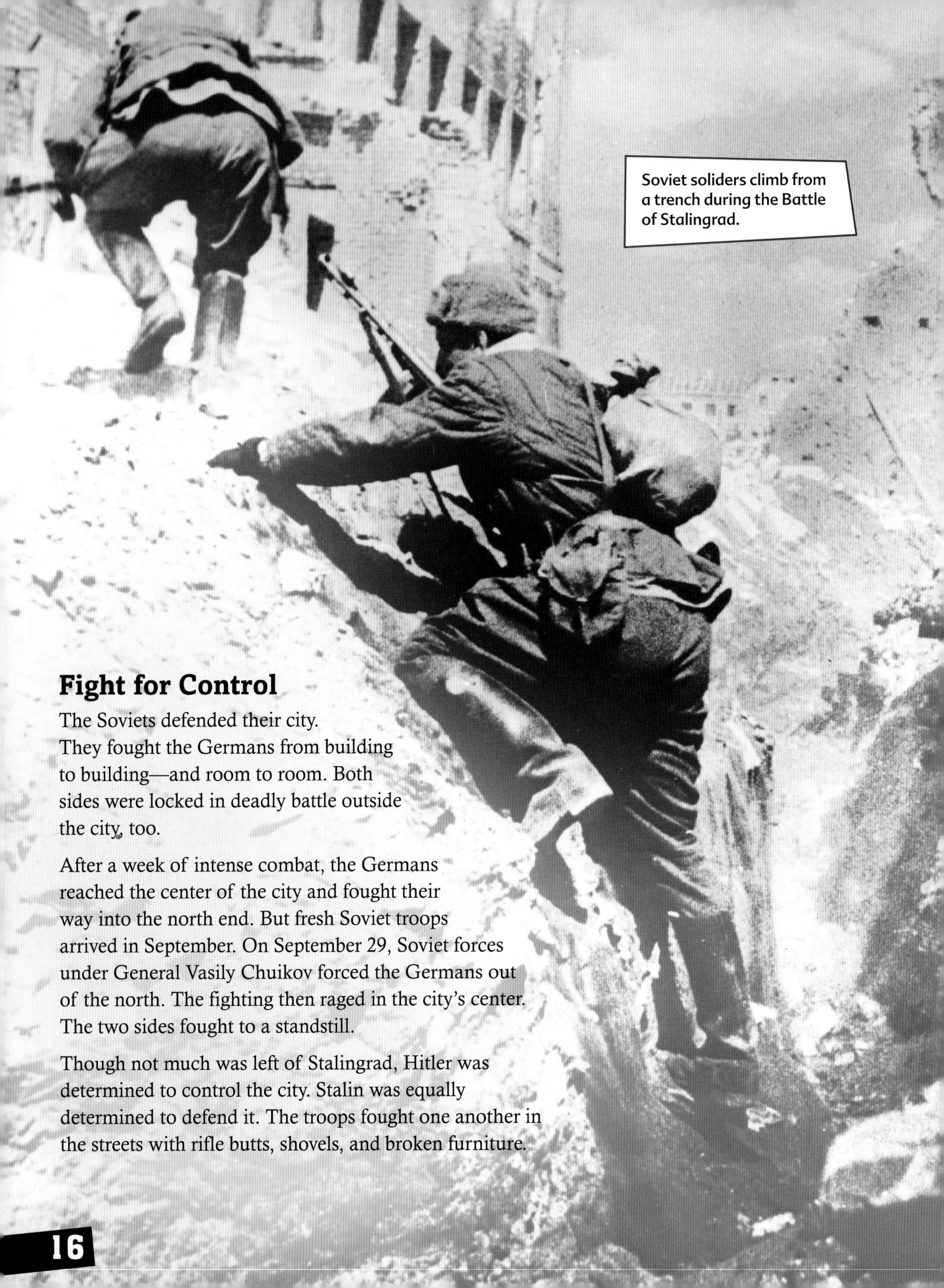

Soviet soliders climb from a trench during the Battle of Stalingrad.

Fight for Control

The Soviets defended their city. They fought the Germans from building to building—and room to room. Both sides were locked in deadly battle outside the city, too.

After a week of intense combat, the Germans reached the center of the city and fought their way into the north end. But fresh Soviet troops arrived in September. On September 29, Soviet forces under General Vasily Chuikov forced the Germans out of the north. The fighting then raged in the city's center. The two sides fought to a standstill.

Though not much was left of Stalingrad, Hitler was determined to control the city. Stalin was equally determined to defend it. The troops fought one another in the streets with rifle butts, shovels, and broken furniture.

Surrounding the Germans

The Russians counterattacked on November 19. The assault caught the Nazis by surprise. The Soviets nearly surrounded Germany's Sixth Army.

Nazi generals pleaded with Hitler to allow the Sixth Army to retreat before the Russians encircled the troops. But Hermann Goering promised Hitler that the Luftwaffe could fly in 500 tons of supplies a day to keep the army fighting. As the Russians closed in, Hitler ordered Paulus to stay put.

Final Surrender

Help never arrived. Goering never made good on his promise, dooming Germany's Sixth Army. The bloody winter battle continued. Combat and cold took its toll on the Germans. They did not have proper clothing or enough food. On February 2, 1943, the German Sixth Army surrendered. Stalingrad was the bloodiest battle of the war with some 2 million casualties. The Soviet victory was the first substantial German defeat in Europe and a major turning point in the war, especially on the Eastern Front.

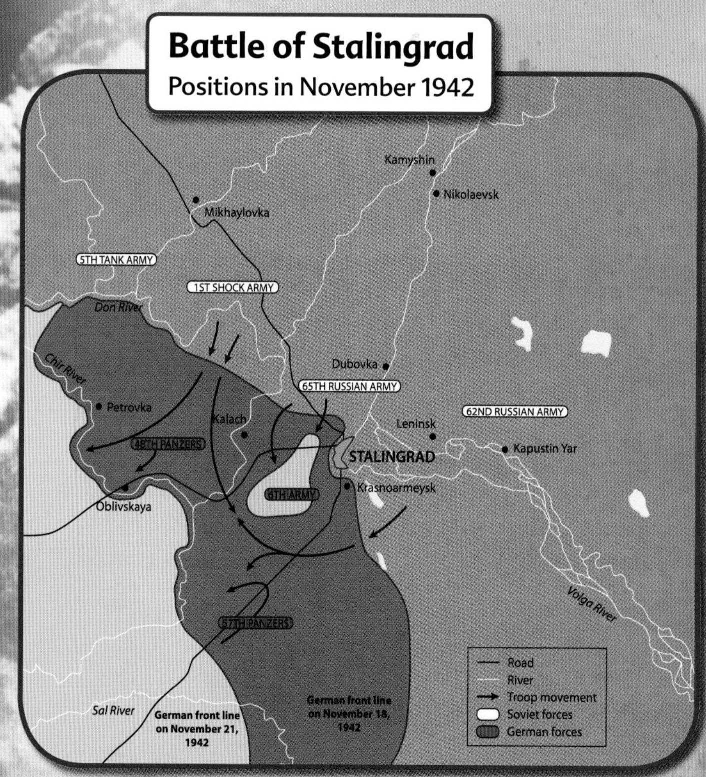

Midway

By the summer of 1942, the Japanese were on the move in the Pacific, conquering the Philippines, Guam, and parts of New Guinea and the Solomon Islands.

Hoping to destroy the rest of America's Pacific fleet, the Japanese eyed a tiny atoll called Midway, located about 1,000 miles from Hawaii. Midway was small, but it was the gateway to Hawaii and the West Coast of the United States.

Japanese Admiral Yamamoto, the mastermind of Pearl Harbor attack, planned to destroy the remaining U.S. aircraft carriers and capture Midway. He sent a small task force as a distraction to attack the Aleutian Islands off Alaska. The idea was to lure the main American forces away from the Japanese battle fleet so that Yamamoto could strike at Midway.

Oil tanks burn on Midway Island.

Plan of Attack

Commander:	Admiral Chester W. Nimitz (United States)
Tactics:	Inflict heavy damage on the Japanese fleet
Where:	Midway Island (North Pacific)
Date:	June 1942

U.S. Navy fighters battle to control the sky over Midway.

Secret Revealed

The Americans, however, discovered Yamamoto's secret plan. U.S. Admiral Chester Nimitz made plans to ambush the Japanese. On June 4, 1942, a U.S. Navy plane spotted the enemy approaching Midway. That morning an air battle began. American dive bombers attacked the Japanese carriers *Akagi*, *Soryu*, and *Kaga*. Fuel and arms on airplanes aboard the *Akagi* exploded as American planes dropped bombs on its deck. The other Japanese carriers burst into flames.

Chester Nimitz, commander of the U.S. Pacific Fleet.

Loss and Retreat

Planes from the Japanese carrier *Hiryu* sank the U.S. carrier *Yorktown*. But the battle forced Yamamoto's task force to limp back to Japan. Japan's loss at Midway was huge. The Japanese navy would never recover. The momentum in the Pacific war favored the U.S. from that point forward.

In Command: Admiral Chester W. Nimitz

Admiral Chester W. Nimitz helped draw up a simple **strategy** to beat the Japanese in the Pacific—"island hopping." American troops would "hop" from island to island all the way to Japan, hitting the enemy at its weakest points.

Invasion of Normandy

For the Allies to win the war, they would have to force the Nazis from Western Europe.

U.S. troops land on Omaha Beach.

By June of 1944, the Allies had assembled the largest naval force in history. The Allies prepared thousands of ships and airplanes to cross the English Channel and invade Normandy, France. If they could successfully invade France, the Allies would be able to push east toward Germany.

General Dwight D. Eisenhower was placed in charge of the Allied forces. Earlier in the war, Eisenhower had led the successful Allied invasions of North Africa and Italy. D-Day, the code word for the invasion of Normandy, would be Eisenhower's greatest challenge.

Plan of Attack

Commander: General Dwight D. Eisenhower (United States)
Tactics: Invade Europe
Where: Normandy, France
Date: June 6, 1944

Dwight Eisenhower, leader of the Allied invasion of Europe

Crossing the Channel

The Allies planned to cross the English Channel and land troops at five beaches along the Normandy coast. The Germans had heavily fortified that region with concrete bunkers, gun batteries, and machine-gun nests. The Germans had littered the beaches with mines, wood, steel, and barbed wire.

Weapons of War: Landing Craft

The Allies used specially made "landing craft" to get troops from the ship onto the beaches of Normandy. One type of landing craft could hold up to 388 troops. Another type could carry four Sherman tanks.

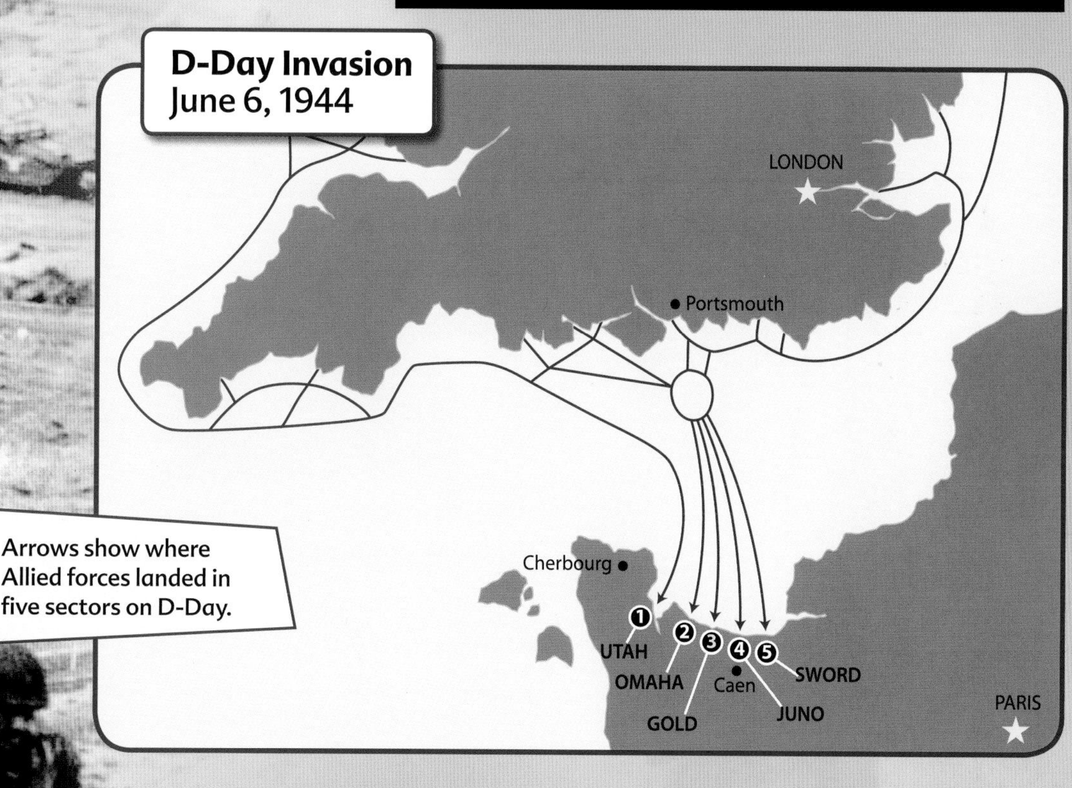

Arrows show where Allied forces landed in five sectors on D-Day.

D-Day was originally scheduled for June 5. But bad weather forced the Allies to postpone the plan until the next day. In the early hours of June 6, nearly 7,000 vessels, including landing craft, began leaving England. More than 800 aircraft took off in the darkness from English air bases to support the Allied landings.

Taking the Beaches

Airborne troops were the first to fight. They dropped behind German lines and attacked enemy targets. At around 6:30 A.M., the first seaborne troops landed. British and Canadian forces stormed the beaches they had code-named Gold, Juno, and Sword. American forces landed on Utah and Omaha beaches. By nightfall, 156,000 Allied troops had come ashore.

Some of the heaviest fighting occurred on Omaha Beach. There, the Americans tried to establish a **beachhead**, but Nazi troops cut them down. With more than 2,000 U.S. casualties, Omaha Beach seemed to be a disaster for the Americans. But commanders rallied their troops and moved inland.

American soldiers land on the coast of France under heavy fire.

Holding Back

At first, Hitler did not believe reports of the Allied invasion. He thought it was a **diversion**. He believed the main attack would happen elsewhere. Rather than send additional tanks to Normandy, Hitler held back. As the battle dragged on, the Germans counterattacked, chiefly around the British and Canadian landing areas. Most of the German tank divisions were bottled up fighting the British and Canadians, making it easier for the Americans to capture a seaport called Cherbourg. The Allies used the seaport to move more troops and supplies into France.

German prisoners are taken ashore on June 8.

The Final Toll

After days of fighting, the Allies broke free from the beaches and moved deeper into France. The Battle of Normandy took a huge toll on every army. All numbers are estimates, but about 320,000 Germans were dead, missing, or wounded. The American losses numbered about 135,000 dead, missing, or wounded; the British, 65,000; the Canadians, 18,000; and the French, 12,200.

The Normandy invasion was the beginning of the end for Hitler and Nazi Germany. Now, the Germans had to split their forces and fight a two-front war.

Battle of the Bulge

After the Normandy invasion, the slog through Western Europe would not be easy for the Allies.

By late 1944, the Germans were fighting the Russians in the east, and the Americans and British in the west. Hitler knew that Germany could not beat the Russians. He decided to launch a **counteroffensive** on the Western front, hoping to force the Allies from the field and possibly win a peace agreement.

In Belgium, U.S. troops march in the snow.

Plan of Attack

Commander:	Generalfeldmarschall Gerd von Rundstedt (Germany)
Tactics:	German counteroffensive
Where:	Belgium
Date:	December 1944–January 1945

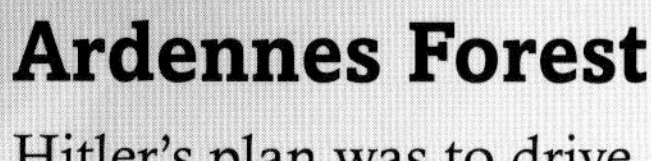

Ardennes Forest

Hitler's plan was to drive a wedge between the advancing Allied armies in the west. The Germans would move through the heavily wooded Ardennes Forest in Belgium. They would try to capture the Belgian port city of Antwerp.

A U.S. tank rolls over snow in Luxembourg in 1945.

Commanded by Field Marshal Gerd von Rundstedt, the Germans used around 1,000 tanks and everything they had. The counteroffensive came as a surprise to the American and British forces, which were already spread too thinly.

Line of Defense

Privately, von Rundstedt believed the German plan was doomed from the start. He did not think that Antwerp could be captured. Four years of worldwide fighting had taken its toll on the German military. There were not enough planes, tanks, or even troops. Young boys and old men were doing most of the fighting now.

Nevertheless, the Germans attacked on December 16 with 250,000 troops across a front that stretched from southern Belgium into Luxembourg. German tanks and infantry rapidly charged through the Ardennes.

Despite snow, ice, and wind, German forces advanced 50 miles into the Allied front lines, creating a "bulge" in the American and British line of defense.

Gerd von Rundstedt, German field marshal

Patton Attacks

The shocked Allies retreated in the freezing cold. Bad weather grounded their planes. But the Americans regrouped. General George S. Patton, head of the American Third Army, attacked the southern **flank** of the Germans. Meanwhile, American soldiers slowed the German advance by holding key roads, bridges, and towns.

By December 20, the Germans had surrounded an American force in the town of Bastogne. When the German commander ordered the Americans to surrender, the U.S. troops refused.

Americans form a roadblock on December 10, 1944.

The U.S. 44th Infantry fights as part of the 6th Armored Division during the Battle of the Bulge.

Rescue Mission

Patton's tanks came to the rescue of the surrounded soldiers at Bastogne.

Elsewhere, as the German tanks continued their advance, they ran low on fuel. The Allies regrouped and counterattacked. By late January 1945, the Germans had retreated.

The actual numbers of casualties are unknown. More than 70,000 Germans died or were wounded in the Battle of the Bulge, according to some sources. More than 70,000 Americans also were killed or wounded. The Germans would never mount a major offensive in Europe again.

In Command: George S. Patton

General George S. Patton was one of the most controversial and effective generals of World War II. Following the Normandy invasion, Patton and his troops advanced across Europe with great success.

General George S. Patton, U.S. commander in North Africa and Europe

Battle of Berlin

As the war drew to its end, Soviet troops advanced from the east and Allied forces approached from the north and west to put the squeeze on Nazi Germany.

By April 1, the Russians were on the outskirts of Berlin, Germany's capital. They built up their forces for two weeks. Then the Soviets began heavy air and artillery attacks. Millions of shells rained on Berlin, a city already heavily damaged by years of British and American bombing.

The Battle of Berlin is fought in the streets.

Plan of Attack

Commander: Field Marshal Ivan Konev (Soviet Union)
Tactics: Capture Berlin
Where: Germany
Date: April–May 1945

In March, the Americans and British shifted their plan of attack away from Berlin. But the Soviets moved ahead with their plan to capture the German capital. The Soviets had two field marshals, Georgy Zhukov and Ivan Konev. Zhukov's army was 50 miles east of Berlin. Konev was about 75 miles southeast of the capital.

The End of Hitler

On April 16, Russian armies boxed in Berlin from the north, west, and south. By April 24, the entire city was surrounded. The Soviets sent about 2.5 million troops, 6,000 tanks, and 40,000 pieces of artillery to fight against the Germans holding Berlin.

Adolf Hitler hid in an underground bunker as 300,000 German soldiers fought for the city. Hundreds of thousands of Russian soldiers, German troops, and civilians perished in the battle. Hitler committed suicide. Germany surrendered. The war in Europe was finally over.

Soviet planes fill the air over Berlin in April 1945.

Okinawa

By spring 1945, the American strategy of "island hopping" had paid off. American troops finally were in a position to invade Japan.

Okinawa, a small island 350 miles southwest of Japan, played a significant role in U.S. planning. Okinawa had an excellent harbor and airfield. It was the perfect place to launch an invasion.

Before any invasion of the Japanese homeland could be attempted, the Allies needed to conquer Okinawa. More than 120,000 Japanese soldiers were defending the island. In addition, there were 10,000 Japanese aircraft ready to fight. The Americans planned to "soften" up the Japanese defenses by bombing from the air and from ships. The waters around the island were cleared of mines to ensure safe passage for ships carrying U.S. troops.

A U.S. battalion readies for battle on the shore of Okinawa.

Plan of Attack

Commander:	Lt. General Simon Bolivar Buckner, Jr. (United States)
Tactics:	Capture Okinawa
Where:	Okinawa
Date:	March–June 1945

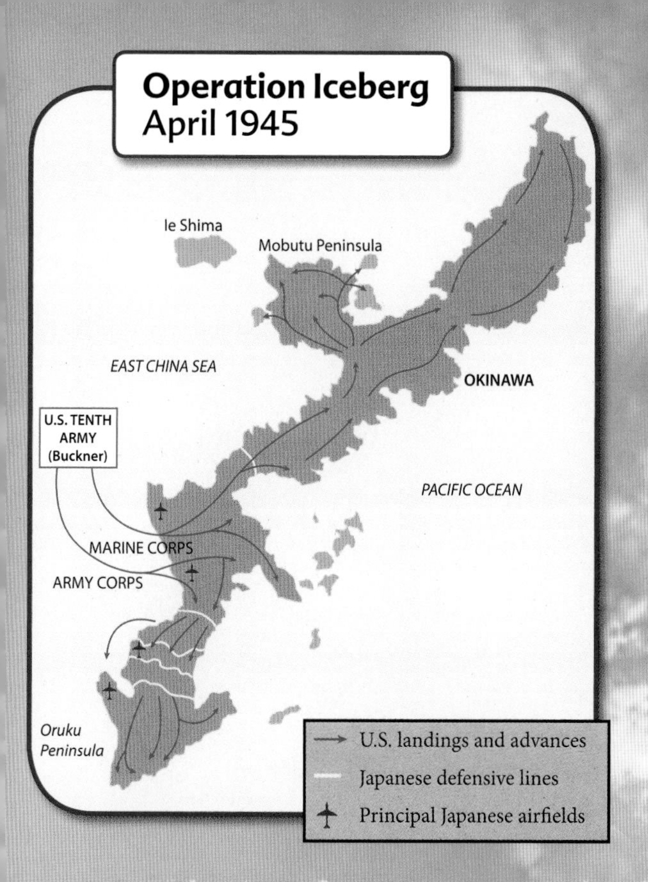

Taking Okinawa

"Operation Iceberg," as the attack on Okinawa was code-named, was set for April 1. That day, 60,000 U.S. Marines and soldiers came ashore. There was almost no opposition at first. But as the Americans moved inland, the Japanese defenders sprang into action. The Japanese fought back hard for 82 long days.

Fight to the Finish

In the northern part of the island, the Americans wiped out the Japanese forces quickly. But the main fighting took place in the south. There, the Japanese were prepared to fight until the last soldier fell. Heavy rain turned the battle into a muddy, bloody mess.

When the fighting was over, the dead Japanese and local islanders numbered about 110,000. General Buckner, commander of the U.S. land forces on Okinawa, was killed. The U.S. reported about 50,000 troops killed, missing, or wounded.

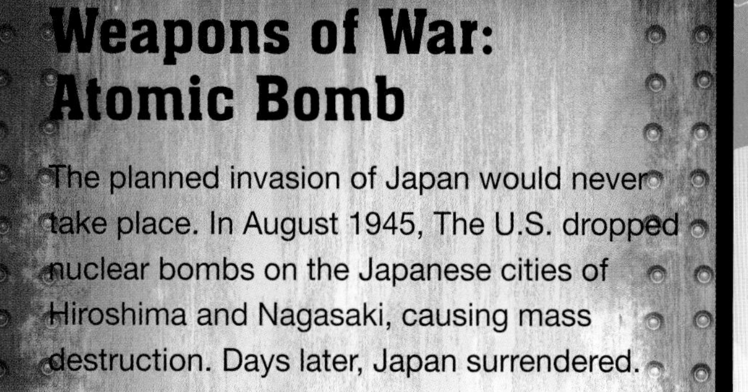

Weapons of War: Atomic Bomb

The planned invasion of Japan would never take place. In August 1945, The U.S. dropped nuclear bombs on the Japanese cities of Hiroshima and Nagasaki, causing mass destruction. Days later, Japan surrendered.

The atomic bomb explodes over Nagasaki, Japan.

Glossary

Allied—of the group of nations, including the United States, Britain, France, and the Soviet Union, that fought against the German, Japanese, and Italian alliance during World War II

artillery—heavy weapons, such as cannons and missile launchers

beachhead—starting position of invading troops on a shoreline held by an enemy

counterattacked—fought back against an attack

counteroffensive—attack by troops that had been on the defense

diversion—distraction

dogfights—aerial battles

flank—the right or left side of an army

occupation—control of territory by an army

paratroopers—troops that go into battle by parachuting out of airplanes

radar—a device that uses electromagnetic waves to identify moving objects such as airplanes or ships

strategy—a plan or approach

task forces—military units with a specific job to do

wolfpacks—nickname given to WWII German submarines that attacked together

Index